Survival Guide

SCHOOL

Survival Guide

Based on the series created by Terri Minsky

New York

Contents

Why YOU Need ME

HI THERE! I'm Lizzie — but you already knew that, right? How was school today — pretty rough? Forgot to hand in your homework? Got hit in the face by three dodgeballs? Totally ignored by your crush-boy?

Let's face it, school is a nightmare — unless you've got the inside track. I learned *that* the hard way.

Lizzie: zero
Total humiliation:
fifty million

Trust me on this, you need a guide to help you get to the end of the week — and that's where I come in!

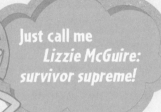

Just call me *Lizzie McGuire: survivor supreme!*

So check out my handy hints for surviving school — I've got it all covered. Ever wonder how to tell if he's *really* crushing on you? Or how to survive science class? How to get through class trips? What to say to Mathletes? And how to avoid dork status? Okay, so maybe I'm still working on that, but I still have plenty to teach you.

First off, it's essential to know who's got your back ... and who's gossiping *behind* your back. Take a look at my list, and think about who *your* best buds are....

The Girls

Name: Miranda Sanchez

Aka: My best bud (along with Gordo, of course!)

Bio: She's clever, she's cool, and I don't think I've ever seen her wear the same outfit twice. Every girl should have a Miranda!

Most likely to say: "I agree — Ethan *is* hotter than a hot, hot thing!"

Least likely to say: "Wow, Gordo! Tell me more about African throat singing!"

Weak spots: Ryan in theater class (he's like Miranda kryptonite). Eating too much flan. And sometimes being just a *teeeensy* bit too sure of herself.

Best moment: Being really cool about the awful review I wrote of her performance in *Greasier*. . . . Well, after she totally flipped out, anyway.

Gotta make up for that acting ability somehow...

Worst moment: Going to the pool party without me. But it turned out okay.

Could surprise you by: Learning to play the violin, and having a pretty great singing voice.

Survival strategy: Cherish her! A good friend is hard to find. She's as necessary as air, water, and lip gloss.

Name: Kate Sanders

Aka: The Queen of Mean

Bio: Kate and I used to be best buds, but it didn't last. Now she's a cheerleader and I'm not. As far as she's concerned, I'm so uncool, I might as well be Mrs. Larry Tudgeman. Kate's got a big head, big hair, big popularity ratings, and a big head. I did mention that she's got a big head, right?

Like, just the once!

Most likely to say: "Hey, nice haircut, Lizzie! Did your mom cut it for you?"

Least likely to say: "Gosh, I sure hope Gordo will ask me out. He's so dreamy."

Weak spots: Ethan Craft

Best moment: Remembering we used to be friends when we had a class assignment on Latvian cooking. Who would have thought an Alexander Torte could bring us together?

Worst moment: Hmm, putting up those posters of Miranda as a dog? Or maybe when her cheerleading squad made up a song about me? Or at Halloween when she made me wear a totally lame clown outfit? Or . . .

Could surprise you by: Forgetting she's the Prom Queen and being nice . . . for one millisecond!

Survival strategy: Ignore her. Popularity isn't everything . . . *is it?*

Name: Lizzie McGuire

Aka: Lizz*eee*

Bio: My motto is, "Life is what happens to you when you're busy being totally humiliated." If my life were a color, it'd be beet red.

Most likely to say: "Come on, ground — swallow me up already!"

Least likely to say: "I just can't imagine life without my little brother."

Weak spots: Are you kidding? Okay, in no particular order: strawberry ice cream, Ethan Craft, detention, Angel Lieberman, Mr. Pettus's breath, cheerleaders, little brothers, unicorn sweaters, rice pudding, class trips, confrontation . . . and conversations with my mom about my feelings.

Best moment: Finally getting up the courage to ask Ethan out on a date . . . attagirl, Lizzie — shoot for the moon!

Worst Moment: Ethan telling me he thinks "we should just be friends."

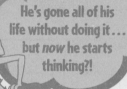

He's gone all of his life without doing it . . . but *now* he starts thinking?!

Could surprise you by: Anything — hey, the sky's the limit!

Survival strategy: Who, me? I'm a pussycat. Everyone knows that!

The Boys

Name: David Gordon

Aka: Gordo. The Gordmeister. Gordzilla. (Last two only ever used by himself. Once.)

Bio: Gordo's not exactly cool, but he's not a geek, either. He knows loads of stuff, and he truly moves to the beat of a different drummer.

Most likely to say: "I'm reading this great book, *The Structural Engineering of Model Bridges*."

Least likely to say: "I have no opinion on that subject."

Weak spots: Monster Truck rallies. And he gets kinda weird about me dating guys... not sure why....

Best moment: For one tiny, beautiful moment, Gordo was the swingin'est cat in the joint when swing music got big at Hillridge. He even gave Ethan tips on how to be cool. He had it *all*.

Worst moment: Swimming around in a sea of rice pudding. No more Mexican quiz shows for him!

Like, yuck!

Could surprise you by: Telling you what you need to know... or possibly just something about Scandinavian leather-industry import taxes. It's a bit of a lottery, to be honest.

Survival strategy: Like fertilizer, Gordo's wisdom is most useful spread thinly, but pretty bad when it's in a *great big heap* in front of you.

Name: Ethan Craft

Aka: Captain Wonderful. My Heart's Desire. Mr. Hottie

Bio: Ethan is *totally* hot. He's the hottest guy in the school. He's so hot he has to wear asbestos pants. But, well, how to put this? It's a good thing he's pretty, 'cause he's not exactly the sharpest tool in the shed.

Most likely to say: "I got stuck in a revolving door yesterday. There was, like, no exit!"

Least likely to say: "Let's go to the library!"

Weak spots: Kate Sanders and her cheerleaders. Hair gel commercials. And words of more than one *syl-la-ble*.

Best moment: Asking me out on a date once! A date! Me! And Ethan! Me and Ethan! Did I mention he asked me out?

I did, right? I did mention that, didn't I?

Worst moment: Any math test. Cute he can do, math he cannot.

Could surprise you by: Announcing that some people are better off as friends... like *us*... AAARGH!

Survival strategy: Ethan's like a cloud — beautiful to look at... just not very substantial.

Name: Larry Tudgeman

Aka: The Tudge. El Tudge.

Bio: You know when something terrible happens, and witnesses say, "But he was such a normal-looking guy"? Nobody would ever say that about Tudgeman.

Most likely to say: "All right — broccoli!"

Least likely to say: "Check out my new designer kicks — aren't they the phattest footwear you've ever seen?"

Weak spots: Actually, *nothing*. Popularity, wearing the right clothes, hygiene — he couldn't care less!

But if he lost his ten-sided role-playing game dice, he'd freak!

Could surprise you by: Showing you it's okay to be yourself — even if you're really weird.

Best moment: Dumping a whole bowl of punch over Kate. Dumping a whole bowl of punch over Kate. (I know I said it twice — I just like hearing it!)

Worst Moment: Eating worms for votes on election day. Yuck! On the other hand, he won!

Survival strategy: Smile nicely, and back away *veeeerrry* slowly.

Friendship Quiz

We all need friends . . . especially at school. It's a jungle out there!

You, Ethan.
Me, Jane?
(*sigh*)

I'm really lucky that Gordo and Miranda have got my back — they're the best! But not everyone's as lucky as me. In fact, some people's "friends" are downright uncool . . . like when Kate hurt her shoulder, and what did her so-called best friend, Claire, do? Totally dissed her, that's what — and then got her canned from the cheerleading team!

So how can you tell if your friends are pals or piranhas?

1 All your friends have started wearing totally cute sparkly tops to class. You really want one, but you can't afford it. What do your friends do?

a) Nothing. They say you look totally cool no matter what you're wearing!

b) Chip in to buy you the top. Helping a friend look good = priceless!

c) Say, "Oh, are you still wearing *that*? *So* last season."

2 The hunkiest guy in the school — who everyone is crushing on — has just asked *you* out on a date. What do your friends say?

a) *Go, girl!* Let's get you ready for the date!

b) Hey, that's really cool… I *guess.*

c) Wow! He picked *you*? Go figure!

3 The big school dance is tomorrow. You've been looking forward to it all year, but you're sick with the flu! *Aaargh!* What do your friends do?

a) Ditch the dance, come over to your house, and rent some videos!

b) E-mail you pix of the dance the following day, and tell you it was no fun without you.

c) Ask if they can borrow your coolest shirt... "since you won't be needing it."

4 Your teacher accuses you of cheating on a test. Only thing is, it was your *friend* who was cheating— you're innocent! What does your friend do?

a) Comes clean immediately — she can't let you take the fall!

b) Pleads with the teacher on your behalf. After all, she's sure you "won't do it again..."

c) Promises she'll visit you in prison.

5 You've gotten friendly with the new kid. She's really nice, but a bit goofy. You introduce her to your friends — what do they say?

a) "Hi, there! Welcome to the neighborhood. Wanna get some lunch with us?"

b) "Hey, see you around, I guess."

c) "Eww, new kid!"

6 You didn't make the cheerleading team, but all your friends did. What do they say?

a) "Never mind, there's always the next tryout!"

b) "Hey, you could always be our water girl."

c) "Gimme an L! O! S! E! R! And *whaddya got…*?!"

Scoring:

Mostly a's: friends forever!

Don't let 'em get away. These are the kind of friends that'll stay with you through thick or thin! They sound almost as cool as Miranda and Gordo. Definitely keepers!

Mostly b's: average buddies

Hmm, not bad. They've certainly got your best interests at heart, though they could try harder. But they're not going to sell you out.

Mostly c's: lower than the lowest

I've got a news flash for you — these buddies are trouble! Are they there for you, or are you just there for them? Better have a rethink, before they freeze you out!

And now, here's my little tribute to the best friend a girl could ever have....

Reasons Why Miranda Rocks

Having a friend like Miranda at school is a surefire way to survive. You just can't make the journey alone! And I'm pretty lucky to have Miranda at my side, because...

- She stands up to Kate...even if I don't.

- She always listens to my problems...and often comes up with good advice.

- She can listen to Mr. Pettus for way longer than I can before falling asleep.

- She doesn't care if she can't act — and she sure can sing!

- I've always got a lunch buddy to sit with.

- Between us, we can just about work out what Mr. Dig is talking about. Kind of.

So that's why *my* best friend rocks... what about *yours*?

My best friend rocks because…

_____

_____

_____

_____

_____

_____

_____

_____

_____

_____

But Does He Really Like Me?

Calculus... world peace... the meaning of life — all *really* easy to sort out, compared to the BIG question: "Does he really like me?"

Hey, you could always just try *talking* to him. (Just kidding. Like, who's gonna do *that*?!) Believe me, I've tried every method to find out if Ethan likes me, and here are some you really *don't* want to use....

Magic 8 Ball

If you don't like the answer it gives you, you can always try again. And again, and again, and again... Let's face it, you could be shaking it all night!

Telepathy

Useless. If this worked, I'd have crushed Matt's mind like a soda can by now. Don't even bother.

Okay, concentrate...
Ethan? Can you hear me,
Eeethannnn?
Goooo out with
Liiizziiieee....

Getting your mom to call his mom

Pretty good if you want to spontaneously combust from sheer embarrassment. Hey, make sure your mom mentions that you're "simply adorable," for the crowning touch.

Asking the kids at school what he thinks of you

I suppose skywriting could be a quicker way of letting him know you're crushing on him, but this is way cheaper.

Passing him a note in class

So second grade! Do you like me? Check one: yes, no, or maybe.

How to Be Popular
Part I

 Be a cheerleader. Duh!

 Have a house with a pool, or failing that, a *really* big TV.

 Have all the brains sucked out of your head with a gigantic straw.

Footnote: Subhuman mutant brothers are a definite no-no.

She's All That...Right?

Sometimes it seems like being popular in school is the most important thing in the world. But is it really all that? I've been popular a few times....

Sure, like, for ten milliseconds.

And there's always a downside. Like, when I was a model, everyone treated me differently. So let's take a look at reasons you might want to be popular — you could be surprised at what it really means....

People like you more — right?

Yeah, maybe, but it's hard work being popular — you have to know a lot of people just a little.

Hey, it's tough being that shallow!

Popularity means that a lot of people know you, but it doesn't mean that they're your friends. I mean, I'm sure Claire doesn't even know what Kate's middle name is! But I know everything about my friends, even Gordo's dorky middle name (Zephyr. *Shh*). Plus, everyone likes to see the popular kids brought down a notch. Remember those creepy Day of the Dead Halloween skeletons, Kate? Quick! Rub some more chocolate cake in your hair to get rid of them!

Popular people have more fun

Well, maybe, but Claire sure does spend a lot
of her time organizing parties and stuff. I mean,
maybe she has fun bossing people around, but
having a rep to keep up has gotta be pretty
tiring. Tudgeman's got no human friends (I'm
not counting the Dwarflord Club) but he has
more fun with his rotisserie baseball and
amphibious skeletons than Kate ever has telling
people what to do, I'll bet. Sometimes I think
popularity's just a big act. (A big, glamorous,
fun act, but an act just the same.)

Popular people are happy

This is so not true. Have you ever seen piranhas on TV? Those guys are nothing compared to how popular people behave if they see someone wearing the wrong *sweater*....

Look, for the last time, it was a present from Gammy!

And if there's nothing to be witchy about . . . they'll turn on each other. Remember when Claire got Kate bumped from the cheerleading team, and Kate had to go to — *gulp* — the dork hall?

Ethan's pretty happy. . . but then Ethan would be happy if you gave him a ball to bounce, so maybe he doesn't count.

So, in conclusion . . .

Worried about your looks? Worried about your image? Worried about your clothes? Worried about your rep? Sounds like a whole heap of worrying. Not worth it!

How to Be Popular

Part II

* Don't try too hard. Popular people are like dogs... they can smell fear.

* Start being so unpopular and uncool that you actually loop around to the other side. (Also known as the Gordo maneuver!)

How to Survive...
Popular Kids

Cheerleaders & Jocks

Jumping around, running fast, and flunking math — you can see why these guys are our natural superiors...

So what makes these high school "royals" tick? Check it out...

Where they hang out: The cafeteria, sports games, the hallway — anywhere people can see them and adore them!

What to say to them: Nothing. Don't speak to them unless they speak to you — you'll only regret it!

What not to say to them: "Don't you worry that your obsession with popularity is actually a result of your deep insecurity? Oh, and by the way, you have something big and green caught in your teeth."

Their idea of a fun night: The same as yours — only *you're* not invited!

Popularity rating: Infinite. (Just don't ask them to give you a mathematical definition of infinity.)

Fashion Kids

They look right, they act right — and they won't do anything unless they've seen it in a magazine.

Where they hang out: In small elite groups in the school yard.

What to say to them: "Hey, check out my new sneakers/jeans/organizer. You can only get these in New York."

What not to say to them: "Nice top. Betty's Bargains?"

Their idea of a fun night: Checking out the new arrivals at the mall... so they can boast about them in class the next day.

Popularity rating: Huge. (As in, "Didn't you know? Plaid is *huge* this season.")

Are You Truly Cool at School?

Being popular at school might *seem* important... but you sure have to hang out with some queen bees! I'm not sure it's worth it. It's better to take a leaf out of Gordo's book — just be yourself.

Be more like *Gordo*? What am I thinking?

Hey, bear with me ... he does what he likes, has fun with his friends, and doesn't care what other people think. That's pretty cool, and way better than being a so-called "popular" kid. So, do you want to just be popular, or truly cool? Answer these questions to find out.

1 There's a "girls ask boys" dance at school, but you'd rather stay in and catch a movie. What do you do?

a) Go anyway — your friends would never forgive you!

b) Watch that movie — your friends can fill you in tomorrow.

2 Would you rather

a) Have everyone at school know who you are?

b) Really know who your friends are?

3 You're having a bad hair day. Do you

a) Pretend you're sick, so you can't go to school?

b) Go anyway, wearing your favorite hat to cover up the disaster?

4 Your popular school friends catch you in front of... a *museum*! What do you say?

a) Oh, hi, guys, just going in to use the restroom. What *is* this place, anyway?

b) Have you seen the rusty old coin collection here? It rocks!

Mostly a's: Watch out, you could end up like Kate!

Mostly b's: You don't care what other people think at school because you're truly cool!

How to Survive...
Double Es

Doesn't matter where you go to school —
every place has got them. They love playing
Dwarflord, solving word puzzles, and
wearing pocket protectors. Whether you
call them geeks or dweebs, Double Es are
everywhere. But how can you tell them
apart? Take a look at my handy guide!

Mathletes

Wow, where to start? Algebra — they love it! Quadratic equations — you betcha! Calculus — all over it! These guys just can't get enough.

Hey, wasn't Dad a Mathlete? Figures!

Where they hang out: The math classroom and the library (checking out the Dewey decimal system).

What to say to them: "How about those integers?"

What not to say to them: "I just heard the Supreme Court made a new ruling, and now π is just three." (They'll explode!)

Their idea of a fun night: Having some friends over for a sleepover, making some popcorn, and counting to a million.

Double E Rating: Infinite. (And they *can* give you a mathematical definition of infinity.)

Chess Clubbers

Sitting still. Planning. Thinking things through real slow. Chess has it all! And these guys love anything to do with chess.

Where they hang out: Nice quiet rooms, or anywhere with a black-and-white tiled floor.

What to say to them: "Chess is the sport of kings!"

What not to say to them: "Isn't this just like checkers — only less complicated?"

Their idea of a fun night: Reading transcripts of historic chess matches.

Kasparov: QKn4

Deep Blue: KnC3

Kasparov: CKn4

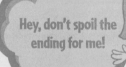

Hey, don't spoil the ending for me!

Double E Rating: Large. (Like their attention spans.)

The Orchestra
(aka the Dorkestra)

Keeping time… obeying orders… endlessly talking about sousaphones… what's *not* cool about the orchestra?!

On the other hand… having a talent other than rhythmic gymnastics would be nice!

Where they hang out: The music room.

What to say to them: "You guys will never guess how much gunk I collected in my spit valve last practice!"

What not to say to them: "Don't you ever get tired of playing the theme song from *Star Wars*?"

Their idea of a fun night: Listening to their favorite album, *Greatest Hits of the Solo Bassoon*.

Double E Rating: Big. (But subtle and musical like the tone of a well-played xylophone. Or something.)

School of Cool: Where Do You Fit In?

Ever wondered where your place is in the scheme of things? Take a look at this useful chart I've created to help you work out your position in the popularity stakes. Check off where you belong!

A chart?
A *useful* chart?
Mr. Pettus,
watch out!

○ **CHEERLEADERS:** Top of the tree. Junior-high royalty.

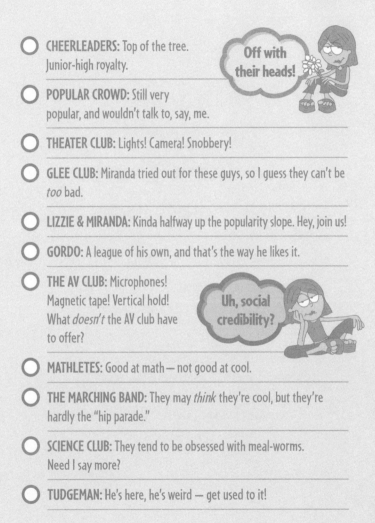

Off with their heads!

○ **POPULAR CROWD:** Still very popular, and wouldn't talk to, say, me.

○ **THEATER CLUB:** Lights! Camera! Snobbery!

○ **GLEE CLUB:** Miranda tried out for these guys, so I guess they can't be *too* bad.

○ **LIZZIE & MIRANDA:** Kinda halfway up the popularity slope. Hey, join us!

○ **GORDO:** A league of his own, and that's the way he likes it.

○ **THE AV CLUB:** Microphones! Magnetic tape! Vertical hold! What *doesn't* the AV club have to offer?

Uh, social credibility?

○ **MATHLETES:** Good at math — not good at cool.

○ **THE MARCHING BAND:** They may *think* they're cool, but they're hardly the "hip parade."

○ **SCIENCE CLUB:** They tend to be obsessed with meal-worms. Need I say more?

○ **TUDGEMAN:** He's here, he's weird — get used to it!

A Scenario too Horrible to Think About

Your little bro attends the same school as you.

This can go one of two ways. Either it's really cool to have a sib at your school, you really enjoy seeing him every day, and he doesn't embarrass you at all...

And then there's what *actually* happens. Most of the time you'd rather listen to Mr. Pettus sing "The Periodic Table Song" than speak to your kid brother at school. (And Mr. Pettus's singing is banned in forty-four states. Look it up!)

For: Okay, so maybe having a younger sib at school isn't *all* bad. You'll always have someone there to talk to, or look after, and you can pass on your excellent School Survival Tips!

Against: If your bro is anything like *mine*, then you don't want him in the same school. Or on the same *planet*.

Mars? Mmm, I dunno, it's too close. Jupiter's nice this time of year, though!

The worst that could happen: He could become more popular than you, make all the kids at your school love him, and then hang with your favorite hottie and freeze you out.

What to do: Hello? Is this 911?

The Teachers

Name: Mr. Dig

Aka: Hey, does he even *have* a first name? Does "Mister" count?

Bio: Our substitute teacher — he substitutes stuff he makes up for the real lesson plan. Fun, though!

Most likely to say: "Okay — I want you to give your book report, but through the medium of interpretive dance."

Least likely to say: "Let's concentrate on the textbook. Then we'll have a test."

Weak spots: Getting off the point. Last week we ended up covering the entire American Revolution… in *math* class.

Best moment: Getting Miranda, Gordo, and me through the Fact-A-thlon… *and* we avoided going to Florida! Kate's still peeling from the sunburn!

> That sounds dangerously like *learning*, McGuire.

Worst moment: Wiping out in front of everybody on his scooter. But he just got up and dusted himself off!

Could surprise you by: Giving you the real deal on life. Mr. Dig lets you tackle problems your own way.

Survival strategy: Just hang on and enjoy the ride!

Name: Mr. Pettus

Aka: Mr. Dweebus (Kate's idea, by the way)

Bio: Mr. Pettus is half science geek and half nerd. But for a guy who sets himself on fire so frequently, he's pretty cool.

Most likely to say: "H_2SO_4"

Least likely to say: "Aw, it's *only* chemistry...."

Weak spots: "The fascinating beauty of the periodic table." Hey, *he* said it!

Best moment: When my mom took the rap for TP-ing the boys' tent on the class trip. Should have seen his face!

Worst moment: Threatening to make me eat a rat on a field trip has to be pretty far up the list! He got far too *Survivor* on that trip, let me tell you!

Could surprise you by: Spontaneously combusting before your very eyes. When Mr. Pettus teaches you about safety in the lab, you better stand back.

The first three rows – you *will* lose your eyebrows.

Survival strategy: Keep your wits about you and a fire extinguisher nearby.

Code Blue!
Assignment Failure!

It happens to the best of us — you get to class, and suddenly you remember you were supposed to hand in your assignment that day!

Um, my brother's chimp ate my homework . . . Or not.

So, what do you do? Do you try to bluff your way out? Or should you just take the rap? There are several ways to deal . . . it's up to you!

1. Get out of class — quick

Remember this rule about getting out of class: the wilder the reason, the quicker you get out... but the more dangerous it becomes! If you say you've got a headache, you might not get out of class at all, but if you say you've just remembered you have to go have experimental brain surgery today, it'll either get you out quick, or get you rushed to the ER!

Good ways to get out of class:

- faking a fainting fit (you might not have to fake it if it's a really big assignment!)

- speaking in tongues

- pretending you just saw a giant bird kidnap Coach Kelly outside (will only work once)

2. Think of an excuse

I'm terrible at excuses — I crack quicker than too much foundation on a hot day. On the other hand, my disgusting little brother is a world-class excuse-maker. He doesn't get many assignments at his school, but he hands them in late on general principle.

Matt's "Top Ten Reasons Why My Assignment Is Late"

- I realized no one would be able to comprehend its genius.

- I did hand it in... metaphorically speaking.

- It caught on fire. Then a dog ate it. Then the dog caught on fire.

- The aliens told me not to hand it in.

- It fell through a time warp... so I actually handed it in last year.

- I've done the assignment in Morse code.
  Here goes —*ahem*—*dot-dot-dash-dot-dash-dash-dot*...

- You're feeling very calm, very relaxed. Now, repeat after me: there *was* no assignment.

- My sister used the paper to write love letters.

- I'm afraid I can't hand in the paper on religious grounds.

- I thought you said October 17, 20*10*.

3. Grovel pathetically

There's only one thing teachers like more than straight, truthful apologizing... and that's pathetic groveling! But only use as a last resort, because it could bring your cool rating way down. For extreme emergencies, here's one I came up with myself:

"Uh, about that, Mr. Coopersmith — I, er, what I mean to say is, my, you're looking so well today, Mr. Coopersmith.... Yes, the assignment — well, uh, I forgot to, er... is that a new cologne, Mr. Coopersmith? Uh, yes well, um, so sorry, Mr. Coopersmith."

Didn't work. Go figure.

Untrue School Facts

Part I

❀ "School" is Latin for "arena of humiliation."

❀ School was invented by Abraham Lincoln in 1860 as a way to use up the nation's oversupply of chalk.

❀ Cafeteria food is 20 percent sawdust.

How to Survive...Class

English Class

Great if you're a huge fan of Shakespeare, but pretty lame if you're not. The best that can happen to you in English class is being asked to read out a part in a play with some totally cute guy as your love interest.

But let's face it — that doesn't happen very often, and usually you're either trying to write a book report on a book you haven't actually read, or having to learn about some book that was written a hundred years ago.

 It's in the past, just let it go!

My advice is to keep your head down, learn your verbs, and hope that you get to play Juliet to Ethan's Romeo!

Music Class

To paraphrase a poet, "If music be the food of love . . . then Ethan's a *symphony*!" Music class is pretty cool, but don't get it confused with the Marching Band, which is *not* so cool. In class you get to listen to a lot of music, which can be fun — even if sometimes that music is Gordo's *African Throat Singers* CD.

Trust Gordo to love music you can only understand with a degree in physics.

Social Studies

This class totally rocks. Why? Well, where else could Miranda get married to Ethan, or Gordo find out that he's destined to be a blackjack dealer, or I learn I should train to be a cosmetologist? Pretty much *anything* can happen in Social Studies…

Fingers crossed for Kate's getting eaten by a dinosaur, then.

…but you need to pick and choose. Learning about who you'll be when you grow up is pretty cool, but learning about the judicial system is strictly for geeks. Hey, but any lesson that can end up with Kate's getting three gallons of cherry punch tipped over her big hair has got to have something going for it!

Mr. Dig: Out There or on the Ball?

Sometimes you actually *learn* stuff in school — I'm not making this up! I mean, most of the time you're supposed to be learning something *else*, but when Mr. Dig is your teacher, you generally end up better informed....

❧ Like when Miranda, Gordo, and I were studying for the Fact-A-thlon, Mr. Dig helped us study in a way that was exciting — not just memorizing lame facts. We didn't win... but we sure had fun learning.

❧ Or like when I became a model — Mr. Dig told me I should go for it, but maybe he really knew I wouldn't like it in the end, so he just let me find out for myself.

❧ Or like on the scavenger hunt — I realized that winning wasn't the most important thing... not if it meant hurting my friends.

Hey — I guess you *can* learn stuff at school ... you've just gotta look for the hidden lessons. They're everywhere. Oh, except algebra — there's nothing to learn there, believe me.

Maybe Mr. Dig isn't as flaky as he makes out. Maybe some teachers are actually interested in helping you learn stuff ... in an exciting way. Maybe he's a man with a plan.

Or maybe he's just really out there. Who knows?!

Lizzie's Study Tips

Part I

No one likes to do it, but sometimes it's gotta be done.

Yeah, they used to say that about using leeches on sick people.

I'm talking about studying. Check out my ideas on how to get the learning done faster so you can get back to thinking about the hottie of your choice....

1. Find a quiet place

If you can't hear, you can't study, so it's best to find a quiet place where you can settle down to work. If you're anywhere near Matt's Mile of Death skateboard track, or Miranda bringing the house down in drama class, or Tudgeman with his *Star Wars* impressions ...

... then it's pretty much a bust. If you're at school, why not try the library? It's real quiet, has tons of books ... and nobody goes there — ever.

2. Cut out distractions

Even if your study spot is a real quiet place —
like the library or the Larry Tudgeman
Appreciation Society — you can still distract
yourself. Definite no-no's include: playing music,
thinking about Ethan Craft, trying to work out
what Gordo was talking about earlier, wondering
what Ethan Craft is doing right now, pondering
why paperboys make really bad boyfriends,
weighing up the pros of learning Spanish if
you're going on a Mexican game show,
wondering whether Ethan Craft is thinking about
you right now, or trying to figure why Brooke
Baker would want to go on a date with Gordo.
Any of that is a bad distraction.

3. Study with a buddy

Studying with a pal is a good way to learn together. You can test each other, help each other, and it doesn't seem so scary, even if you've got lots to do. Friends can make studying just about bearable. (But, hey, Mr. Pettus, it's never gonna be "the most rewarding thing you'll ever do." Nice try.)

You've gotta choose your buddy carefully... it's a minefield out there!

- ❋ *Not* someone you're secretly crushing on — studying and crushes don't mix. It'll end up either a lousy study session... or a *really* lame date.

- ❋ *Not* someone you can't understand half the time — like a certain Mr. Gordon.

- ❋ *Not* someone you have too much fun with — you can make it interesting, but it's not a sleepover party!

- ❋ *Not* your little brother — too young to help ... not old enough for reform school. Avoid.

- ❋ *Not* someone who's going to go off to summer camp — and then come back with a big 'tude and start dissing you for no reason.

- ❋ Not dad's cousin Ree-Ree — because he lives in Minneapolis. What a weird suggestion....

Coping With Being...
an F Student

"Omigosh! That's it! Stick a fork in me — I'm done!" These are some of the things you might be thinking if you get an F. But it's not the end of the world!

Sometimes getting an F can be a good thing — it can make you want to do better next time, or highlight that there's something you don't understand about the subject. Look at it as a warning signal, do something about it, and move on. And if *that* doesn't cheer you up, just think about what good company you'll be in... after all, Ethan is no stranger to the occasional F.

Coping With Being...
an A Student

What? Am I for real? There are problems with being an A student? Gimme a break! Well, yeah — there can be! Just because you get straight A's (like Gordo) doesn't mean your life's perfect. And it's not a guarantee that you'll become popular around school, either (like Gordo).

Good grades are important, but you don't want to wreck your life getting them. So if your life is getting swamped by the pressure of grades, and you're feeling overwhelmed, why not talk to a good friend about it? Like Gordo!

Lizzie's Study Tips

Part II

Set goals for yourself

Studying can be tough — especially if you have to research the national dish of Latvia on short notice…

Latvia? Didn't he win Wimbledon last year?

…but you can break up the study time by setting yourself goals. Try to get something finished before rewarding yourself with a break, or getting a snack — stuff to look forward to, like:

- having a soda

- taking a walk around the house

- marrying Ethan Craft

- transporting your kid brother to the Phantom Zone

- having a number-one hit

- meeting Brad Pitt

- eating a tuna melt

Instant Genius!

Okay, so you need to impress a teacher, and quick! What do you say? No problem — I'm on the case. Throw these into your class conversation and you'll sound like Einstein. Just make sure you get the timing right, that's all!

English: "This passage has a very *Joycean* feel to it, Mr. Coopersmith."

Math: "Yes, but that solution can only work in *non-Euclidean* mathematics, of course...."

History: "I'm not sure studying by timeline helps — I like to take a more *holistic* approach to history."

Gym: "Can I do *more* laps, Coach Kelly?"

Places Not to Study

The bowling alley

Too crowded, too stinky... plus, you might get distracted by the sound of one of your friends having a panic attack because of his irrational bowling alley phobia.... Avoid.

Your local coffee shop (like the Digital Bean)

This sounds like a good idea, but then it's... "just a cappuccino, please"... then... "and a muffin"... plus, a little... "oh, hey! Is that Ethan talking to Kate over there?" Way too distracting!

The cafeteria

You might get some work done here, but you also might get real queasy from the smell of cafeteria cheese.

Untrue School Facts
Part II

* You spend more than eight million hours in school during your lifetime.

* Hall monitors are worthy of your respect.

* Gym teachers are well-rounded individuals with lots of friends.

The Day of Reckoning

Aka: Parent-Teacher Conference Night!

I study hard, I have Gordo help me with the difficult stuff, and I hand my assignments in on time. Well, almost always on time. But I never know what the verdict will be on Parent-Teacher Night.

Whether it's a good report, or a bad one, you should always be prepared. So take a look at my survival guide to Parent-Teacher reports.

If your report is bad...

☀ Deny everything your teachers said about you. Keep denying it until you're eighteen and leave for college.

☀ Say... "D's are the new A's — you are so last year, Mom!"

☀ Stare at your folks real hard and chant: "You are veerrry happy with my report. Veeeerrry happy..."

☀ Tell your folks the school is built on top of a giant underground magnet, and it wiped out your memory.

☀ Say, "It's because of all the lead in the cafeteria lasagna."

☀ Say, "I know I got bad grades — but I've been learning to do *this*!" Then start dancing like a crazy person.

If your report is good...

☀ Say, "A good report is its own reward... but about that *car*..."

☀ There will never be a better time to talk about getting your belly button pierced.

☀ Suggest that it's time for your little brother to go to military school. Leave a brochure for your folks to read.

☀ Suggest you finish with school "on a high note" and start working as a model.

Cheater, Cheater, Pencil Eater!

Okay, let's get serious here for a second. At some point in your school life, you're gonna get the opportunity to cheat on a test, or maybe help someone else cheat. So you wanna hear my survival tip for this scenario? Listen up real good, 'cause I don't want you to miss this.

Don't do it!

Why? Here's why: it's a lose–lose situation! You either get caught or you get away with it, and neither's good. The only time I cheated on a test, I helped Angel "Doberman" Lieberman out... and I got busted! I got sent to detention, too, and had to lie to my mom about where I was. For a while I was so off base, I even *hung out* with Angel Lieberman!

And that's just the *best* result! Because even if you're not caught, you start to feel guilty (like I did when the principal's statue got busted and the Spring Fling was canceled… and I didn't even *do* it!). Pretty soon you're gonna start thinking about smuggling yourself to Tibet and starting your life over as a yak herder.

Believe me — it's not worth it. So next time you get the chance, just think: what's worse… getting a C on the test, or only talking to yaks for the rest of your life?

Just you and the herd.

Take a Chill Pill!

Studying can be tough — especially when you've got two assignments to hand in, and you have a sneaking suspicion there's going to be a pop quiz in the afternoon. But getting stressed is only going to make things worse.

Try to unwind by:

Breathing deeply

Sounds lame, but it really can help, and you can do it anywhere. More air to your brain helps you think better and stay chilled.

Taking a walk

Just moving around helps, and can take your mind off your worries. Just don't walk straight out of school!

Having something to look forward to

Think, "Okay, so I've got that quiz, but this evening me and my buds will rent a movie." Give yourself a cool goal to reach for!

Faking It

Now, this is something I never do, but there are times when you just *can't* go to school. Whether you're wearing a unicorn sweater, or have a giant zit on the end of your nose . . .

Pulling a sickie rocks! Woo-hoo!

. . . faking an illness is the only way to go. Now, personally, I'm not a good faker, but I am related to one of the fakiest kids there is. Check out the stuff I've copied from Matt's *Notebook of Doom*. . . .

Matt McGuire's Guide to Faking It:

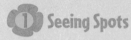 Seeing Spots

You will need:

1 red felt-tip pen
1 shortsighted mom

Method:

Apply the felt-tip pen to your face, creating a dotted effect (don't forget your eyelids!). Then groan and say you've got any one of the following:

- Chicken pox
- Measles
- A terrible rash

Helpful tip:

Don't overdo it and claim you have *small*pox. They will take you away and burn all your stuff.

Success rating:

Pretty good. But it does depend on how thick your mom's glasses are....

 **Gimme Fever**

You will need:

1 lamp with working lightbulb
1 thermometer

Method:

Tell your mom you have a headache and a terrible
temperature (remember, no one can *check* for headaches!).
When her back's turned, take the thermometer out of your
mouth and hold it against the lightbulb* just for a split
second. Instant high reading!

Helpful tip:

Don't overdo it and leave it there for five minutes. No one
will believe a fever of 250° — you are not a human torch.

Success Rating:

It's 100 watts of pure brilliance!

*Make sure it's *on* first!

③ The Old Switcheroo

You will need:

The acting skills of Robert De Niro

Method:

In the morning, ask your mom for a ride to school, because "I feel really weird and headachy today but I don't want to miss school." Every time she asks if you're okay, say that you're completely fine — then sigh heavily and blink lots. Don't forget: you *want* to go to school....

Helpful tip:

Don't overdo it and start saying stuff that no one would ever believe, like "I've just *gotta* get to school and take that algebra test... I've just gotta!"

Success Rating:

Hmm, could go either way — either a bust from the get-go, or a surefire cinch. Nothing in between.

How Not to Phone in Sick

Of course, I'd never normally do this, but if it were an extreme emergency — like Matt dyeing my hair blue — I might have to consider it.

Me: "Hello there, good morning. I'm afraid Lizzie McGuire won't be in school today — she's sick."

Teacher: "Oh, I'm sorry to hear that... and who is this speaking, please?"

Me: "Umm, this is my father speaking."

Me: "Hello, this is the president of the United States calling. Just to let you know, Lizzie McGuire is on a top-secret mission for me and won't be in school today."

Teacher: "Oh, *really* — what's your middle name, Mr. President?"

You: "Er, I don't know. Good-bye! Don't forget to vote!"

Dodgeball:
Fun Game or Painful Ordeal of Terror?

Dodgeball should be banned under international law. Until it is, here's some information that might help you get out alive:

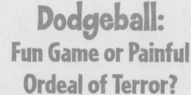

- Dodgeball was invented during World War I as a way of making prisoners confess.

- The greatest number of simultaneous dodgeball hits was six — sustained last year by one Larry Tudgeman of Hillridge Junior High. Doctors say he may still not be right in the head.

- If you rearrange the letters in "dodgeball" you get "dead ball." Well, almost.

- Coach Kelly is wanted in more than seventeen states for dodgeball-related crimes.

- The only way to survive a dodgeball game intact... is not to play.

Field Day

Now, I like *some* sports — I'm pretty good at rhythmic gymnastics, actually! But there are a few sports I *don't* like (pretty much anything suggested by Coach Kelly). One big area you've gotta watch out for is Field Day. Why? Let me spell it out:

- lots of competitive sports
- the whole school watching you
- . . . and judging you
- . . . and mocking you
- your mom and dad being there

Hel-*lo* — recipe for total humiliation! I'd rather square dance with the Tudge again!

My advice is to sign yourself up for stuff that won't embarrass you to death, like...

The Egg-and-Spoon Race

No pressure, no one takes it seriously, and no one cares if you look dumb! (Because who *doesn't* look dumb balancing an egg on a spoon?)

The Triple Jump

So boring that no one will want to watch it. You're safe!

A Relay Race

Just make sure you're not on the last leg, and then no one will blame you if you lose!

Or why not try my personal favorite: don't actually participate at all! All you have to do is sit on the sidelines and cheer — no problem! And the great thing about being on the sidelines is that you can watch all the hotties getting hot and sweaty.

What's that? Ethan's in the swim race? HOLD THE PHONE!

How to Survive...
Class Trips

What to do if... your mom comes along!

Wow, tough spot! Not only is your mom coming along, which is pretty embarrassing, but she'll also be kinda acting like a teacher *and* — gets worse — trying to "talk to your little friends." Total humiliation! Be warned: she may even try to "talk the slang" with them.

Survival tactic:

Relax! Getting uptight won't help, and your classmates might start to tease you if they see you're embarrassed. So what if your mom's there — she's pretty cool, really!

Class Trips to Museums

The Museum of Pop Music, the National Center for Cute Boys, or the National Accessorizing and Sleepover Museum — these are all places that your teacher *never* takes you to. No — instead, say hello to fossils, coins, broken pots, rocks, charts, and really old bottles.

Must... stay... awake...

Survival tactic:

Every museum has a gift shop and a café — even the really lame ones! If you've got an assignment to do, team up with friends to get it done quicker... then go shopping!

Survival no-no:

However, be selective. Don't buy stuff in the gift shop just 'cause you're there — hotties do not dig "I went to the Kalamazoo Museum of Cheese!" T-shirts. Trust me.

The Great Outdoors

Ahh! The great outdoors!
Fresh air!
Trees!
Flowers!

Bears!
Snakes!
Rain!

Believe me — you should fake an illness rather than go on a camping trip, where the whole of nature is against you . . . and that's *before* your teacher goes psycho and makes you eat rat for dinner. (Well, almost.)

Survival tactic:

Find shelter, and fast! First, get those tents set up — find some boys to do it (they've gotta be useful for *something*, right?). Once you're cozy in your sleeping bag, open up the snacks and start spinning those ghost stories. What, you didn't know this was an *ancient Indian burial site*. . .? **Whoooo . . . *whooooo*!**

Class Trips to the Theater

Well, the theater can be kinda fun, but it depends on what you're seeing. (If the title is *Greasier*, starring Miranda Sanchez... run for the hills!)

Survival tactic:

Don't get too depressed if it turns out you're going to see a really old play, like Shakespeare or something — deep down, most of them are pretty interesting, with love stories, sword fights, and even the odd joke!

Hey, I'm not making this up — *Gordo* told me!

So you *could* end up having fun after all. Just don't fall asleep when the lights go out!

Survival no-no:

Don't throw rotten fruit at the actors. That stuff stains.

Teacher's Pet?
Nope — Yours!

Every school has a pet, and some are luckier than others. Some get to be taken home by a nice family, looked after, pampered, and sent back to school with a smile on their snout.

And some school pets get looked after by Matt. We buried his school's pet lizard . . . on the first day he looked after it.

I mean, how can you tell if it's alive or dead, anyway?

As you can imagine, that earned him a really bad rep at his school. Survival moral here? Don't look after school pets — if they roll over on you, your reputation takes a dirt nap, too.

If you're asked to pet-sit… watch out! Pets you certainly *don't* want to look after include:

- stick insects
- a hamster with an eating problem and a weak heart
- any type of poisonous toad
- a dinosaur
- a rattlesnake
- an elephant
- an electric eel
- a mayfly (guaranteed not to last the week!)
- any kind of animal that can get itself lost, wedged under the floorboards, into the garden, or stuck in the microwave

The Cafeteria:

A Nice Place to Visit, but Hold the Cheese!

The cafeteria is: a place to hang out; somewhere you might get to see how cute Ethan's looking; a place to avoid Kate; or just somewhere you can go and watch Tudgeman try to eat three pounds of Jell-O.

The cafeteria is not: somewhere you should eat. But just in case you do, here's the 4-1-1 on what's good to eat, and what should hit the street....

Good

Apples

These are pretty safe. No cooking involved so not even the lunch lady can get it wrong. But make sure you wash it first, just in case.

Broccoli

Anything that's been boiled that much has gotta be clean. Right?

Packaged Cookies

Protected from all the elements!

Water

This is okay — if it's been boiled.

Bad

Hamburgers

Are you kidding me? Those things are made out of mystery meat — if you're lucky. Stick to your favorite burger place, like the excellent Digital Bean.

Jell-O

Hell-*lo* — were you listening earlier? Tudgeman's favorite food, and it's made from horses' hooves. Ew!

So, the cafeteria: come for the company, leave before you accidentally eat something.

Cafeteria Etiquette

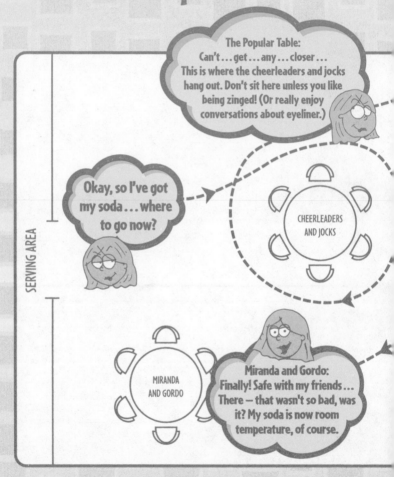

You think going to the cafeteria is easy? Think you can sit where you want, talk to who you want? Think again, my friend! Take a look at my handy diagram to reveal the pitfalls of cafeteria choreography.

MATHLETES

The Mathlete Table:
These guys are harmless, but don't let the Popular Table see you talking to them or you'll be marked for life. Smile, nod, and keep walking....

The Science Club Table:
Same deal as the Mathletes Table. It's instant bad karma if you sit down here, so keep going....

SCIENCE CLUB

The Teachers' Table:
What are you — nuts? No one will like you if you sit here. Especially not the teachers. Pass by, and try to look like you're not doing anything out of the ordinary.

TEACHERS

Tudgeman:
Oh no! It's Tudgeman! He won't let me pass unless I tell him what Jar Jar Binks's middle name is. I take a wild stab at "Jar," and move on quickly....

Shall We Dance?

What is it with my friends and school dances? Either I can't go to the Spring Fling, 'cause I'm taking the rap for Kate's busting that statue of the principal . . .

Hey, you kids! Cut that out!

. . . or Gordo gets turned down by Parker McKenzie when he asks her to be his date, because he's too short . . . or I ask Ethan to a dance, and he turns me down — *twice*!

School dances are bad news! You get all nervous about asking someone out, and even if they say "yes," then you're nervous for the whole week beforehand. If you really want to ask someone to go, here are a few tips:

- Remember, your date is probably just as nervous as you are.

- Don't try too hard to impress your date — just be yourself.*

- Don't drink the punch. It'll be horrible, and you'll get it on your outfit. Yuck.

- If Ethan Craft comes onto the dance floor, watch out for his arms . . . and legs. . . .

- How tall you are doesn't matter — it's how much fun you are to be with! (Right, Gordo?)

- Even the popular kids are nervous at school dances — remember, they've got reps to defend!

   * (If you're Tudgeman, *don't* be yourself.)

Eww,
What Is That?

No matter what school you go to,
every school has its own weird
odor — one that doesn't smell
quite like anything else on earth.
Ever wondered where it comes
from? Here's my guess:

- cafeteria food

- the sweet smell of success coming off the popular kids

- Tudgeman's socks (when he *wears* socks)

- Ethan's cologne

- the charred remains of Mr. Pettus's lab coat

- Mr. Coopersmith's smouldering good looks

- the stench of defeat from our basketball team

- Monday morning blues

Lizzie McGuire, Survival Guru, Signing Out

So there you go — my crucial guide to surviving school! It's been real. And, hey, it must be working so far because you're still reading! Keep this book with you at all times — you never know when you might need it. But if you only remember one thing, it should be this: if you've got good friends around you, and you know who you are, then you'll never go wrong.

Oh, yeah, and Ethan's phone number. That'd help, too!

So best wishes, best foot forward, and remember — no matter how embarrassed you might be at times, at least your pants never split, showing the whole class you were wearing "Tuesday" underwear (on a Wednesday).

If by any chance this book hasn't helped you survive your school, you can always get a transfer to Hillridge! Miranda, Gordo, and I will look after you. (Just remember to duck when Kate comes around the corner!)

Catch you later —

Love,

Lizzie